Quotes From The Soul, To Help Heal A Queen's Heart

~

31-Day Inspirational

DANIELLE BAILEY

Copyright © 2017 by UNQLY MADE, LLC: First Edition, 2017

All rights reserved. No part of this book may be produced or transmitted in any form or by any means, electronic or mechanical, including photocopying, recording or by any information storage and retrieval system, without written permission from the author, except for the inclusion of brief quotations in a review. All biblical quotations and scriptures marked KJV are taken from the KING JAMES VERSION (KJV): KING JAMES VERSION, public domain.

Library And Archives Canada Cataloging- in Publication Data

Danielle Bailey Quotes From The Soul, To Help Heal A Queen's Heart; 31-Day Inspirational

Cover Desgin by: UNQLY MADE, LLC
Published by: UNQLY MADE, LLC

ISBN-13:978-0995859401
ISBN-10:099585940X

DEDICATION

I dedicate this book to all the women who has ever gone through abuse, heartbreak, brokenness, insecurities, betrayal, and disappointments, or for anyone who has ever felt less than. Those things and situations that happened in your past though unfortunate, they are not the end all, be all. They do not define you as a person, as a mother, daughter, sister or friend. You are beautiful, You are loved, You are a Queen.

Foreword

There is a queen inside of every woman. Pain does not discriminate, neither is it concerned with race, social economic status or culture. Every woman will experience pain at some point in her life. Too often we dress our wounds with bandages and never allow ourselves to go through the healing process. We are constantly pouring into others, but never allow our spirits to be refueled or restored. Life will take us on a journey that we were never prepared for, however what does not kill us makes us stronger. The pressure, pulling, pain and problems prepares us for our promise. Danielle Bailey has allowed God to pour into her as she listened to his voice for the words of healing to restore his daughters through this book. I am extremely honored to write the foreword for such a powerful and uplifting piece of creative work. I pray that every hand that touches this book will be healed, delivered and set free as they walk in royalty. Let the restoration begin. SylindaD Founder of Removing The Bandages Women Movement

CONTENTS

1. Title Page

2. Copyright Page

3. Dedication

4. Foreword by Sylinda Mumphery

5. Acknowledgments

6. Introduction: Healing Wounds

7. Closing Scripture

8. Poetic Prayer

9. Final Thoughts

Acknowledgments

I first and foremost give thanks, honor, and praise to my Heavenly Father; Yeshua Hamashiach.
It is because of his grace, mercy, love and favor why I am able to minister to these courageous, strong, and amazing women.
I'd also like to thank my beautiful children for putting up with me working long late nights and my saying, "just five more minutes", and last but not least I'd like to acknowledge everyone that encouraged and believed in me from the very beginning, I appreciate you and your support.

Yours Truly,
Danielle

Introduction: Healing Wounds

In this book, I talk about overcoming adversity and challenges in life, while highlighting the common factors we face among other women. Often times we pretend to be jovial and content, but instead, we're content in a comfortable facade. This inspirational book, "Quotes From The Soul, To Help Heal A Queen's Heart: 31-Day Inspirational". Was inspired by the unction of the Holy Spirit to captivate the hearts, minds, and eyes of the women who are in need of a pick-me-up and spiritual encouragement. Wearing a bandage over our battle wounds won't cause them to heal, but rather seal in the infection as opposed to the allowing of a diagnosis of brokenness, heartbreak, insecurities, and worthlessness and receive a prescription of hope, laughter, love, beauty, reassurance, peace, security and wholeness. Christ is made strong in our weakness.

Day 1

Dear Queen,

God is preparing you for new things; but you have to want what God has for you, by being willing to let go of those people, places and things that serve you no good.

Moral: You have to know that, God has plans to prosper you, not to harm you. Everything that the Lord does is always on purpose, for a purpose. Nothing he allows or does will be wasted.

Bible Verse: Wherefore come out from among them, and be ye separate, saith the Lord, and touch no unclean thing; and I will receive you. 2 Corinthians 6:17

Write your thoughts down to express how the daily quote made you think or feel. Then reflect on them to see what you can do to make a change.

Day 2

Dear Queen,

Never allow the perception of others to dictate your present, by the views of your past, when the visions of your future are so promising.

Moral: Often times people will hold onto what they remember about your past, instead of embracing who you've become. That has absolutely no bearing on what God has said about you. Keep on, keeping on.

Bible Verse: Remember ye not the former things, neither consider the things of old. Behold, I will do a new thing; now it shall spring forth; Shall ye not know it? I will even make a way in the wilderness, and rivers in the desert. Isaiah 43:18-19

Write your thoughts down to express how the daily quotes made you think or feel. Then reflect on them to see what you can do to make a change.

Day 3

Dear Queen,

Sometimes no answer is still an answer and though we may prefer to hear a Yes from God, even a No, is still a blessing.

Moral: A "yes", is a blessing from God and so is a, "no". God's "no", is not a rejection, but redirection and protection.

Bible Verse: Furthermore we have had fathers of our flesh which corrected us, and we gave them reverence: shall we not much rather be in subjection unto the Father of Spirits, and live? Hebrews 12:9

Write your thoughts down to express how the daily quotes made you think or feel. Then reflect on them to see what you can do to make a change.

_____
_____
_____
_____
_____
_____
_____
_____
_____
_____
_____
_____
_____
_____
_____

Day 4

Dear Queen,

It doesn't matter what those negative naysayers have to say, as long as you believe in yourself and what God says, then nothing else should take precedence.

Moral: Never fall victim to the opinions of other people. We can do all things through Christ who strengthens us. There isn't anything that we can't do, because with God all things are possible.

Bible Verse: For do I now persuade men, or God? Or do I seek to please men? For if I yet pleased men, I should not be a servant of Christ. Galatians 1:10

Write your thoughts down to express how the daily quotes made you think or feel. Then reflect on them to see what you can do to make a change.

Day 5

Dear Queen,

Who you say you are to yourself is what other people will begin to believe. Speak about yourself in a way that the Lord speaks of you.

Moral: Always speak life over yourself and your situation.

Bible Verse: Set a watch, O Lord, before my mouth; keep the door of my lips. Psalm 141:3

Write your thoughts down to express how the daily quotes made you think or feel. Then reflect on them to see what you can do to make a change.

_____
_____
_____
_____
_____
_____
_____
_____
_____
_____
_____
_____
_____
_____
_____
_____
_____
_____
_____

Day 6

Dear Queen,

You may face hardships from time to time because we all face trials and tribulations. However, you have to remember that when you go through it, you must also grow through it.

Moral: Trouble doesn't last always, and neither will yours. There are times when we will go through the storms of life, but there's also a silver lining, a rainbow to look forward to.

Bible Verse: For his anger endureth but a moment, and in his favor is life; weeping may endure for a night, but joy cometh in the morning. Psalm 30:5

Write your thoughts down to express how the daily quotes made you think or feel. Then reflect on them to see what you can do to make a change.

Day 7

Dear Queen,

Without tests you would have no testimony and without the mess there would be no message to be heard by someone who's waiting to hear your story.

Moral: There's power and purpose in your testimony, God has assigned specific people to you and your life. Your testimony has the power to break chains and free those of them that are in bondage.

Bible Verse: And they overcame him by the blood of the lamb, and by the word of their testimony; and they loved not their lives unto the death. Revelation 12:11

Write your thoughts down to express how the daily quotes made you think or feel. Then reflect on them to see what you can do to make a change.

Day 8

Dear Queen,

You can't afford to listen to what the world has to say, it'll cost you. However, if you would just be still you will always hear the priceless instructions that the Lord gives.

Moral: Anyone can tell you anything that you may want to hear, but that doesn't mean that it's God inspired. Prayer is the only way you can seek the Lord for your answers. Be patient and wait.

Bible Verse: Be still, and know that I am God: I will be exalted among the heathen, I will be exalted in the earth. Psalm 46:10

Write your thoughts down to express how the daily quotes made you think or feel. Then reflect on them to see what you can do to make a change.

Day 9

Dear Queen,

The power of the pain is in the power of the anointing.

Moral: The anointing attracts attacks. So, if you're being attacked it means that you are being elevated, positioned, and promoted into a new level. A new dimension in God's favor.

Bible Verse: Beloved, think it not strange concerning the fiery trial which is to try you, as though some strange thing happened unto you But rejoice, inasmuch as ye are partakers of Christ's sufferings; that, when his glory shall be revealed, ye may be glad also with exceeding joy. 1Peter 4:12-13

Write your thoughts down to express how the daily quotes made you think or feel. Then reflect on them to see what you can do to make a change.

Day 10

Dear Queen,

As a child of God you are already wealthy, the kind of wealth that can't be found in banks.

Moral: True wealth cannot be found in any financial institution, but in eternal life with the Father in Heaven. The things on earth are only temporal, even the trees and grass will wither away.

Bible Verse: Set your affection on things above, not on things on the earth. Colossians 3:2

Write your thoughts down to express how the daily quotes made you think or feel. Then reflect on them to see what you can do to make a change.

Day 11

Dear Queen,

No matter what happens in life always keep your head up, you will prevail.

Moral: We all know that the teacher is silent during a test, but that doesn't mean that he isn't paying attention. Keep pushing, and praying.

Bible Verse: Strengthened with all might, according to his glorious power, unto all patience and long-suffering with joyfulness. Colossians 1:11

Write your thoughts down to express how the daily quotes made you think or feel. Then reflect on them to see what you can do to make a change.

Day 12

Dear Queen,

A real friend will love you with the love of Christ, teaching and be learning how to properly be there for you in times of need.

Moral: No matter the distance of geographical locations the hearts are closer than ever, because love knows the distance, not restrictions.

Bible Verse: Beareth all things, believeth all things, hopeth all things, endureth all things. 1 Corinthians 13:7

Write your thoughts down to express how the daily quotes made you think or feel. Then reflect on them to see what you can do to make a change.

_____
_____
_____
_____
_____
_____
_____
_____
_____
_____
_____
_____
_____
_____
_____
_____
_____
_____

Day 13

Dear Queen,

It's perfectly okay to be perfectly imperfect, know who's you are and who you are. Don't forget that you're fearfully and wonderfully made, uniquely constructed, and fashioned by the potter's hand.

Moral: There's nobody else like you in the world. God is so incredibly meticulous in his creations he didn't need a duplicate.

Bible Verse: I will praise thee; for I am fearfully and wonderfully made: marvelous are thy works; and that my soul knoweth right well. Psalm 139:14

Write your thoughts down to express how the daily quotes made you think or feel. Then reflect on them to see what you can do to make a change.

_____
_____
_____
_____
_____
_____
_____
_____
_____
_____
_____
_____
_____
_____
_____
_____

Day 14

Dear Queen,

A strong woman of God possesses a very peculiar type of faith unlike any other she confounds the faithful with her childlike faith. That's when giants fall and mountains are cast into the very sea she swims in. Possibilities are endless with the God she serves, opportunities are present at every single turn. Like a lion she roars, I am more, as she walks through those God opened doors.

Moral: Keep your faith strong regardless of what life throws at you. You are brilliant, beautiful and bright.

Bible Verse: Now faith is the substance of things hoped for, the evidence of things not seen. Hebrews 11:1

Write your thoughts down to express how the daily quotes made you think or feel. Then reflect on them to see what you can do to make a change.

_____
_____
_____
_____
_____
_____
_____
_____
_____
_____
_____
_____
_____
_____
_____

Day 15

Dear Queen,

You are a wonderful, loving, kind, blessed, anointed individual and even though life can be difficult, please know that you are loved and never forgotten.

Moral: Never give up on being the amazing person that you are, despite what may transpire there are people that love and care about you, Jesus loves you.

Bible Verse: The Lord is nigh unto them that are of a broken heart; and saveth such as be of a contrite spirit. Psalm 34:18

Write your thoughts down to express how the daily quotes made you think or feel. Then reflect on them to see what you can do to make a change.

Day 16

Dear Queen,

The anointing on your life is what is incredibly attractive to him. It's not so much about the physical that piques his interest, but for the simple fact that he sees you operating in your gifts.

Moral: This God fearing man will love all of you, flaws and all because he knows a good thing when he sees it.

Bible Verse: Who can find a virtuous woman? For her price is far above rubies. Proverbs 31:10

Write your thoughts down to express how the daily quotes made you think or feel. Then reflect on them to see what you can do to make a change.

_____
_____
_____
_____
_____
_____
_____
_____
_____
_____
_____
_____
_____
_____
_____

Day 17

Dear Queen,

You'll never have to worry about being battered again, 'nor do you have to return back to that abusive situation.

Moral: You are loved and protected by the Most High, your heavenly father will not allow you to be hurt by them ever again.

Bible Verse: Fear thou not; for I am with thee; be not dismayed; for I am thy God: I will strengthen thee; yea I will help thee; yea, I will uphold thee with the right hand of my righteousness. Isaiah 41:10

Write your thoughts down to express how the daily quotes made you think or feel. Then reflect on them to see what you can do to make a change.

Day 18

Dear Queen,

There will be times when it will get extremely tiring and trying, but do not grow weary. You are much stronger than you give yourself credit for.

Moral: Things can and will get hard sometimes, but that doesn't give you the excuse to give up and fold. Trust in the Lord to turn it around. Have faith and know that he will.

Bible Verse: But they that wait upon the Lord shall renew their strength, they shall mount up with wings as eagles, they shall run, and not be weary; and they shall walk, and not faint. Isaiah 40:31

Write your thoughts down to express how the daily quotes made you think or feel. Then reflect on them to see what you can do to make a difference.

Day 19

Dear Queen,

When someone easily gives up on love, you know that they gave up on lust.

Moral: Don't get so caught up with the facade, some men will show you genuine interest while there are others who will genuinely waste your time. It really wasn't love, it was lust that ran out.

Bible Verse: Flee also youthful lusts: but follow righteousness, faith, charity, peace with them that call on the Lord out of a pure heart. 2 Timothy 2:22

Write your thoughts down to express how the daily quote made you think or feel. Then reflect on them to see what you can do to make a difference.

Day 20

Dear Queen,

If something happens where they suddenly distance themselves and it wasn't warranted, please understand that God intentionally removed them.

Moral: We serve an intentional God, everything that happens in our lives God either purposes it to happen or allows it.

Bible Verse: Be ye not unequally yoked together with unbelievers: for what fellowship hath righteousness with unrighteousness? And what communion hath light with darkness? 2 Corinthians 6:14

Write your thoughts down to express how the daily quotes made you think or feel. Then reflect on them to see what you can do to make a change.

Day 21

Dear Queen,

Stay consistent and loyal to the call on your life, God has a plan.

Moral: Not everyone is going to believe in your dreams or visions, but that doesn't mean that they aren't sent from God. Everybody isn't going to support you and believe you, and they don't have to, just make sure that you are being obedient to what the Lord told you to do.

Bible Verse: There are many devices in a man's heart; nevertheless the counsel of the Lord, that shall stand. Proverbs 19:21

Write your thoughts down to express how the daily quotes made you think or feel. Then reflect on them to see what you can do to make a change.

Day 22

Dear Queen,

Tearing down and building back up is a part of the restoration. There are times in life when God will shake our lives up so that things that are not of him can fall away.

Moral: It is in this time when you will need to fully trust and depend on God to rebuild you, strengthen you and fashion you where you were once weak and susceptible. He will take great care of your heart once you give it to him, because apart from him we are nothing and can do nothing.

Bible Verse: If thou wert pure and upright; surely now he would awake for thee, and make the habitation of thy righteousness prosperous. Job 8:6

Write your thoughts down to express how the daily quotes made you think or feel. Then reflect on them to see what you can do to make a change.

Day 23

Dear Queen,

Your heartbroken days are over if you want them to be over. Walk away from anything or anyone that doesn't serve or meet your highest good.

Moral: I know that we've all heard the saying, "it's easier said than done", but is it really easier said? Truth be told, it can be done. You have to know that you deserve to be treated with dignity and respect.

Bible Verse: For I reckon that the sufferings of this present time are not worthy to be compared with the glory which shall be revealed in us.
Romans 8:18

Write your thoughts down to express how the daily quotes made you think or feel. Then reflect on them to see what you can do to make a change.

Day 24

Dear Queen,

A real man of God looks at the things concerning the heart and the kingdom, not the mere physicality that will eventually fade.

Moral: True beauty does not lie in features of the face, rather in the conditions of the mind, heart and spirit.

Bible Verse: Favour is deceitful, and beauty is vain: but a woman that feareth the Lord, she shall be praised. Proverbs 31:30

Write your thoughts down to express how the daily quotes made you think or feel. Then reflect on them to see what you can do to make a change.

_____
_____
_____
_____
_____
_____
_____
_____
_____
_____
_____
_____
_____
_____
_____
_____

Day 25

Dear Queen,

A real Queen isn't worried about her future King's bling, but rather his anointing.

Moral: The real attraction should be because he's on fire for God, and having a heart after the Lord. The fact that he has vision and purpose, not merely what he possesses.

Bible Verse: And he said unto them, Take heed and beware of covetousness: for a man's life consisteth not in the abundance of the things which he possesseth. Luke 12:15

Write your thoughts down to express how the daily quotes made you think or feel. Then reflect on them to see what you can do to make a change.

Day 26

Dear Queen,

There is absolutely nothing wrong with choosing to remain pure or celibate and abstain from sexual impurity.

Moral: There are no men that are worth selling yourself short or going to hell for. Nevertheless, they don't deserve to have you share your innermost treasure, 'you'. Wait until you've met and married the one God ordained for you.

Bible Verse: But seek ye first the kingdom of God and his righteousness; and all these things will be added unto you. Matthew 6:33

Write your thoughts down to express how the daily quotes made you think or feel. Then reflect on them to see what you can do to make a change.

_____
_____
_____
_____
_____
_____
_____
_____
_____
_____
_____
_____
_____
_____
_____
_____
_____

Day 27

Dear Queen,

Abuse of the body can visibly be seen, but abuse of the mind can only be experienced from within.

Moral: Physical bruises may heal and scars might be left, however that does not equate to the internal emotional damage that will take years to carefully repair.

Bible Verse: The Lord trieth the righteous: but the wicked and him that loveth violence his soul hateth. Psalm 11:5

Write your thoughts down to express how the daily quotes made you think or feel. Then reflect on them to see what you can do to make a change.

_____
_____
_____
_____
_____
_____
_____
_____
_____
_____
_____
_____
_____
_____
_____
_____

Day 28

Dear Queen,

Think it not strange when people come up against you, sometimes their betrayal is your survival to your next coming promotion.

Moral: The fire came to fortify you, not vilify, or victimize you, but strengthen and recondition.

Bible Verse: When thou passest through the waters, I will be with thee; and through the rivers, they shall not overflow thee: when thou walkest through the fire, thou shalt not be burned; neither shall the flame kindle upon thee. Isaiah 43:2

Write your thoughts down to express how the daily quotes made you think or feel. Then reflect on them to see what you can do to make a change.

_____
_____
_____
_____
_____
_____
_____
_____
_____
_____
_____
_____
_____
_____
_____
_____
_____

Day 29

Dear Queen,

Don't you know who you are and who's you are? You are the daughter of the Most high God, the King of King's and Lord of Lord's.

Moral: You can do all things through Christ who strengthens you.
We have power and dominion to tread upon the lion and the cobra; you will trample on the great lion and serpent.

Bible Verse: For I know the thoughts I think toward you, saith the Lord, thoughts of peace, and not of evil, to give you and expected end. Jeremiah 29:11

Write your thoughts down to express how the daily quotes made you think or feel. Then reflect on them to see what you can do to make a change.

Day 30

Dear Queen,

The things of old are becoming obsolete and desolate, whereas your future is looking far brighter, prosperous and vital.

Moral: Don't allow what you see to persuade you into believing that this is what it will always be like. Change is inevitable.

Bible Verse: Thou, which hast shewed me great and sore troubles, shalt quicken me again, and shalt bring me up again from the depths of the earth. Psalm 71:20

Write your thoughts down to express how the daily quotes made you think or feel. Then reflect on them to see what you can do to make a change.

Day 31

Dear Queen,

The chains have been broken, and you have finally been set free. Don't look back at what you lost, but instead look forward to what you've gained.

Moral: When you allow your body rest up you will begin to heal, recover and be restored. Take the time you need, so that when new love or opportunities present themselves you'll be able to openly receive it.

Bible Verse: For your shame ye shall have double; and for confusion they shall rejoice in their portion: therefore in their land they shall possess the double: everlasting joy shall be unto them. Isaiah 61:7

Write your thoughts down to express how the daily quotes made you think or feel. Then reflect on them to see what you can do to make a change.

_____
_____
_____
_____
_____
_____
_____
_____
_____
_____
_____
_____
_____
_____
_____
_____

CLOSING SCRIPTURE

Isaiah 61:1-2

1 The Spirit of the Lord GOD is upon me; because the Lord hath anointed me to preach good tidings unto the meek; he hath sent me to bind up the brokenhearted, to proclaim liberty to the captives, and the opening of the prison to them that are bound; 2 To proclaim the acceptable year of the Lord, and the day of vengeance of our God; to comfort all that mourn.

POETIC PRAYER

I pray that you'd welcome the Lord into your lives if you haven't done so already, it will be the best decision you will ever make. Knowing that you have the gift of salvation and no condemnation in Christ there's preservation; choose to be free from the enemy's temptations.
In Jesus name I pray, Amen.

FINAL THOUGHTS

I hope and pray that over these last thirty-one days you have begun to transform and renew your minds in complete wholeness; as you begin opening up your heart to healing, love, and full restoration. May the goodness of the Lord and God's grace continue to keep you and order your steps onto the new path and journey that you're about to embark. He will lead you through the trials and tribulations that you will face, not leaving or forsaking you, but rather watching over you every step of the way. Please know that you can call on him at anytime he will never miss your calls, press ignore or send it to voice mail; instead he waits for your petitions and prayers seeking to commune with you as he continues to knock at the doorway of your heart. Allow him to make beauty for ashes, I charge you to be bold, and daring; go forth and inspire others along the way.

ABOUT THE AUTHOR

Danielle Bailey is a mother, poet, writer and entrepreneur. However, her passion is helping people recognize their potential, while realizing their worth. Danielle has a powerful testimony in all areas of her life. She's a minister and founder of UNQLY MADE Ministries International. Her message transcends barriers with it's deep healing and impacting delivery that sparks change, encourages deliverance and inspires breakthroughs in the body of Christ. Whereby it exceeds beyond the four walls. Her mission is to breakdown strongholds, and build-up strong souls. She is truly emulating the epitome of what, "Married to Ministry", is all about.

BOOKS BY DANIELLE BAILEY

Quotes From The Soul, To Help Heal A Queen's Heart: 31-Day Inspirational

Poetics- A Prophetic Poetry Devotional: On Life, Love, and Relationships To Help Keep You Spiritually Fit!

www.ingramcontent.com/pod-product-compliance
Lightning Source LLC
Chambersburg PA
CBHW020020050426
42450CB00005B/560